AF413281

A MAN'S LOVE

A MAN'S LOVE

A Poetry Collection

MORALES

I dedicate this book to my Mother, Dad and my two sisters.
Also, to Jeanine, Julianne and Shawnte.
Thank you for your inspiration.

All of these poems were written at the time of pure emotion. Therefore, please be warned. Some of these poems are explicit.

Proofread by Shanwte Carter
Cover art created by Jedzel Estrelloso

I

THE ONES I LOVE

This part is a collection of poems dedicated to various people in my life that I loved. I also included some poems I wrote for other couples I admire. I believe all relationships, romantic or not, are important. I hope you enjoy them.

To everyone who has affected my life, thank you. This collection could not have been completed without you.

PROMISES

I stare into your eyes, kissing your lips
You stare back into mine, smiling a bit
Our breaths match each other's pace
I hold your hand and grab your face
I admire the beauty that you've graced
You tell me you love me and lick my chest
I say I need you and bite your neck
Our hearts fit perfectly together
I'll sacrifice my being to be with you forever
When I'm with you I feel nothing but perfection
Insecurities and doubts leave when I'm your selection
Swear to be your lover and your protection
I see you standing in front of me at a church
Making promises to never hurt and treat each other with worth
As we walk away, there's nothing the world can say
To convince me not to give you my all, day after day

EXPECTATIONS

When you're mine, I'll make all the time
Drinking wine but you're the one that's fine
Holding my hand as we walk the night
You stand in my sight; it just feels right
Our lips meet, you close your loving eyes
One hand on your back, one on your thigh
I never felt more alive
I promise to protect your heart
From my flaws and others
You may cry, but you'll never suffer
I love your attitude and your mental
Follow my fingers around your body like a stencil
My touch runs deep, into your soul
I promise to never be cold
I'll be there to hold, never leave you alone
Take off your shirt and get comfortable
Nibble your ear and massage your muscles
Take your time, enjoy it, I'll never rush you
I love you

SHAWNTÉ

All my life I was crawling towards the light
Surrounded by darkness, it won without a fight
Insecurities and mistakes were thrown in my face
Stuck and lost, no escape
After years wasted on the wrong girls
Convinced no one was for me
After fighting my demons, picking up what I fumbled
A light so subtle shines through the rubble
It was you
Never felt this supported
Never felt this loved
One smile and my heart was healed
Sadness can no longer make me kneel
Thanks to you.
Completely open and honest about all my flaws
And yet you stay.
Told you about my mistakes
Yet you stay.
Love and affection are how I will repay
I'll stay until the end of my days

COMFORT

Had a long day at work
Got into a fight, got some ketchup on my shirt
Felt insecure, lost, sad, and immature
Came home, tears swelling up feeling a disgrace
Then I looked up and saw your beautiful face
You hug me close, tell me I'm alright
I kissed your hand, laid by your side, and talked all night
You tell me I'm the man I need to be
But I feel like I can be better
My head cradles your chest as you rub my scalp
You tell me all the things I do for you, and you kiss my mouth
I grab your hand and unbutton your blouse
I would never make the mistake of treating you any different
I'll always be deliberate, considerate, never ignorant
To your wants and your needs
My hand travels from your chest to your knees
I hold you closer, say I love you and we both fall asleep

LOVE

You're the one that makes me spend my time
My heart shines when you tell me you're mine
Nothing I wouldn't do if you needed to hear I love you
After I show it, I'll say it too
Put in all the effort just to make you happy
I can be a little hard-headed and a little sappy
But I'll kiss you from head to toe, make you moan
As long as I'm here, you'll never feel alone
I'll buy you flowers and listen to you for hours
Massage your neck, tell me how was work
Caress your chest, bite your lip, and feel your breath
Kiss your stomach to your legs, you know what's next
Just want to please you, show you I need you
Give me a chance and my heart is yours
Love and compassion, you never have to worry
I can cuddle with you all night and listen to your stories
Never a question. I'll always be there
This is just an example of the love we could share

ANOTHER MOTHER

A good mother is hard to find, but I have two.
I can't trust most people, but I can trust you.
Hug you whenever I get the chance.
Mark Anthony's playing, care for a dance?
Writing this poem to express my love.
For my second mother, thank you.
Thank you for always being there.
Thank you for your advice, and your care.
I wish I could show my appreciation more.
For a woman who always opens her heart and her door.
You showed me love and responsibility.
I'm hard-headed, you always knock in sensibility.
Thank you for your love.
Thank you for treating me like your son.
Thank you.
I love you, Titi Betsy.

THE WOMAN I WANT

Explaining what I want is a tricky endeavor
I guess I just want a woman to make me better
Not in a way where I need her to survive
But, to comfort me, love me, and never lie
One to hold me when times are tough
Loves me gently and kisses me rough
One that's worthy of my poems and effort
One that's honest and doesn't take advantage
Physical touch is my love language
Holding your hand, walk side by side, let everyone know
I'm your man
Don't believe in something, get mad and take a stand
I need someone strong when I'm weak
Someone loud when I'm meek
Classy and a freak, this is what I seek
Use my heart as stand but my face as a seat
But maybe I'm asking for too much

DREAMS

A lot of my recent poems were about the physical
So typical, I'm having problems being lyrical
Especially, when it comes to how you make me feel
Because it's tough to write about something that isn't real
I know what I can bring to you, pleasure and effort
Sex running through my brain, making my head hurt
It weighs on my heart knowing you don't exist
So, I spend my nights lost in my thoughts
Thinking about all I can give
I want love, marriage and a kid
But it seems like I'm destined to be alone
What am I doing wrong, why am I stuck writing this song?
My heart is jumping in my throat
Really thought I found you a couple times, but nope
Am I a joke?
Regretting every word I ever spoke
Don't get me wrong, I don't want pills or a rope
But what is life without love?
Maybe I'm overthinking
I have close friends, but no lover so I'm over drinking
How does this end? I'm lost...
Stuck, filling this page with pointless thoughts.

ROSE

Circus Roses fit you perfectly
They're hard to find, still looking for one currently
When I first saw you, I was overwhelmed by your physical
attributes
Your beautiful stride, caring face is absolute
But you're much deeper than that, no dispute
The way you listen with no interruption
The way your intentions show no corruption
Makes me think about you constantly
Inspires my feelings into poetry
I understand how this poem can be perceived
But I promise, I am not naive
We are friends
You simply make me believe, a hope that never leaves
That I'll find a woman half as great as you
One that is almost as kind and almost as true
Sometimes I think in another life, things could be different
But I'm glad to have you in this one, you make a difference
Saying any man would be lucky to have you is wrong
Because you're not a prize
You're someone that every human being would love to have by
their side

ANNOYING

We grew up together
Survived the weather in this crappy world
Watched you grow from a brat to a happy girl
I look up to you even though you're younger
Maybe that means I wasn't a good brother
You made it through adulthood without my help
I look back at the times I've hurt you to find myself
The past few years we've been stronger
I guess that's because I don't mess up any longer
Well, at least not with you personally
I promise purposely you'll never be hurt around me
I found me; you've mercifully accepted me permanently
You're the strongest person I know
Thank you for learning from my mishaps
I sit back, one day you'll look up to me, perhaps
I love you

COMING HOME

Randomly smiling at the sweet nothings you said
At work, replaying it over and over in my head
On my way back to you, my heart tightens
Call you, your familiar voice strikes me, my body tingles like
lighting
You tell me you love me, I say it back, as I travel ahead
Get home, no wait, take you, embrace you, and push you onto
the bed
Look you deeply you in your eyes and kiss you first
Kiss your cheek, bite your ear, and take off your shirt
Trace my lips from your chest to your naval
I would give you my soul if I was able
Your attraction is fatal, pleasure you until you're unstable
Your legs finally wrapped around my neck
My heart beating out of my chest
Is this the feeling of lust or love?
Right now, I feel the latter
But it doesn't matter, I move faster, your body, I'll flatter
Kiss your inner thighs, remind you that your mine
And I'm yours, have you begging for more, until your body's
sore
Don't worry, we have plenty of time to explore
I promise I'll always love you down to the core

GOOD MORNING

We wake up face to face
You have work, but I want you to stay
I speak to you with sweet words
I start kissing your lips, with my hand on your curves
I want to start your morning right, I'm here to serve
I want to give you everything you deserve
Every single day you bless me with your beauty
It's my duty to love you and please you absolutely
I trace your body with my hands like a line of chalk
I want to make sure you have trouble trying to walk
My kisses move down, we're close as I remove your clothes
Don't worry about returning the favor
It's all about you, your flavor I savor
Lately we've been bickering but now your legs are quivering
My heart knows what you want
Your legs grow tighter as I capitalize my font
You have my soul, I love you whole, I'm out of control
You finish multiple times I'm on a roll
My hand reaches your breast, my heart beats out of my chest
Your pleasure is my priority, no need for a request
My tongue is stressed, so no need to express the rest
You get up shaking, that was one of hell of an awakening
I tell you I love you; you have to get ready for work
But make sure you give me a kiss first

LEECY

Want to start this off by saying
Leccy I'm sorry
I wasn't there
I promise, unlike my father I care
I was still a child when I found out that you existed
He wasn't around, tried to get close but he resisted
I was a troubled kid, my mother got tired of my shit
So, she dumped me on father's doorstep
Your mother already had two kids, so I added to the mess
He used to take all her money and food and give it to me
Tryna act like the father we know he could never be
We bonded during that time and watched rescue pets
My mother finally took me back and I left
I remember crying because I didn't know when I'd see you next
A few years past with no contact, I was 18 , "daddy" nowhere to
be seen
Thought being "legal" made me a cool, so I started acting up
Dropped out of school, so my mother started packing up
Sent me back to him I was happy, smiling and laughing up
Only if I knew
He was living with a new woman at the time
She was in DR, for 4 months he gambled all their money and
didn't pay any bills
Came back, saw me there, and that was the last straw
This is why not everyone should be doing it raw
We ended up in a hotel, he spent the whole time taking it out on
me
He lied to your mother and said he was getting a house fixed
So, she let you visit

I picked you up from school, you were crying, had a bad day
But then you saw me and all that went away
You jumped in my arms, and we got to know each other
You lost your father, but you gained a brother
I got my GED and moved back
I didn't know life moved so fast, that time would be our last
Fast forward, I became a grown man. Still fucking up
Couldn't keep a job, doing drugs. I was selfish
Wanted to see you but I was helpless.
Finally got out of that and saw you on my Birthday
It went well but I messed up and wasn't consistent
Now you're pregnant. It's crazy, isn't it?
I begged to be in your life for days and hours
Now I can't even afford to come to your baby shower
I'm a failure, there is no more to say
Except that I will fix this one day.

FROM ALPHONSE TO ANNIE

Waiting forever, until we get up above
But it's worth it, because I'm flying high with the one I love
Lately life's been a mess, filled up with stress
I can't wait to hold you in my caress
We finally get to bed, we lay and I stroke your head
I hold you in my arms, my heartbeat slows
My breath speeds up as you take off your clothes
My hand lightly traces your legs up to your neck
Kiss you again, my touch reaches your chest
I'm a man, not a beast, but you're my beauty, my princess
My insecurities build up sometimes
But I let it go, when I know I was chosen
I bring you closer, our bodies remain frozen
I'm sorry if I ever made you feel less than perfect
These past 5 years, in your presence has been worth it
I can't stand to be without you for a second
I make mistakes, but I'll always show effort
I'm a collector and your smile is my greatest treasure
I promise to focus on your heart, goals and your pleasure
Every trip we take makes us closer
Your soul I move toward, no direction but forward
I can go on and on and on, and you know that's what I do
So, I'll end this by saying those simple words. I love you

FROM MIKE TO EVON

Over the years my heart suffered from erosion
I show you devotion but it's hard to show emotion
I never had the luxury of a woman showing me love
You know my mother and the others, it's hard
I guess part of me believes that one day you'll just leave
So, what's the point?
I do love you, from my heart to my joints
You have to understand the kind of man I am
Me taking you to work
That means I love you
Me cleaning the house, washing your shirts
That means I love you
Me picking up every phone call
That means I love you
Me picking you up every time you fall
That means I love you
Every time your son calls me daddy
That means I love you
It's hard for me to express in gifts or words
It's easy for me to stress and leave words unheard
But that's the only love I know.
I'll be with you as long as you'll have me
You know if you ask anything from me I'll do it gladly
So, all I'll ask from you is the benefit of the doubt
Even if I get upset and shout
Even if it's untold.
That I love you with every inch of my soul

MY FAVORITE LOVE STORY

The one thing I can't deny, is my parents love for one another
The year was 1992, my dad walked out of the bodega
The streets filled with cars honking, peoples stomping, and
songs from *La Mega*
They locked eyes and started chatting
My mom was feeling him, eyes batting, Dad jokes had her
laughing
Merengue playing through the speaker as I started to play with
his sneaker
My mom knew at that moment that she was no longer hopeless
She found her soulmate.
He became the man that knows me.
The man that loves me.
The man that chose me.

II

CONSEQUENCES OF LOVE

I spent a long time in my life not loving someone that I should have from the very beginning, myself. Heartbreak, disappointment, feelings of loss, and self-doubt are all part of the journey to love yourself, family, or your partner. This collection of poems will describe a time of depression, the darkness that surrounded me for years. It drove me into alcohol and drugs. I was filled with resentment and anger. Although this was the worst version of myself, it was still part of my journey, and it made me a better person.

CYCLE

I'm controlled by emotions and not facts
Always want someone that don't want me back
It's a cycle that repeats, Brain says want, heart says need
And people wonder why I still smoke weed
Because I'll die with this devotion to commotion
I smoke so I can shut off this emotion
Trying to do better, trying to focus
Let my heart get the best of me and I know this
Always holding on to a slither of hope
A pen and a smoke are the only way to cope
Maybe I'm just weak, a lonely stray that never hits its peak
A coward to pointless discussions so I'd rather write than speak

OVERWHELMING

Hype that I got a girl's number, but she doesn't respond
Smoking in a park and throw my heart in the pond
Making wishes that never come true
I know you all know what I'm going trough
Got my own place, but behind on the rent
Staring at the all the messages left on read
Is there an end?
I'm not really lonely, I have friends
But why does it feel like I'm still alone?
31 and no children to call my own
I know I'm a man, so I'm supposed to be tough
No ring or kids, they say that's a woman's problem
A man is supposed to bottle all his issues and find a way to solve
them
But how much do you think I can hold in?
My soul, heart and mind, I sold them
Abandoned by my father, first lesson of disappointment
Therapist calling me for a missed appointment
Progress, regression, and rejection
the cocktail of my depression
Marijuana killing brain cells and emotions
But it's the only way I can survive this commotion
No metaphors and similes just real shit
If you ever wanted to commit suicide but was afraid to, you'll
feel this...

DRAMATIC

All my life I've been bluffed out
Was showed the light of love before it was snuffed out
Only few will understand that feeling of constant rejection
False promises of a selection, then dropped without a mention
It makes me nervous when people tell me they want me
Because shit never happens
They just be playing
I'm nothing but entertainment
Don't believe me? Let me tell you my stories
Just a look inside my head, don't want you to feel sorry
It all started with Rose
She was petite, sweet and had a cute nose
On my birthday she pulls me aside
She tells me she had a surprise
Kisses me and tells me I'm the one she likes
Heart was so high, felt like I was riding a sunrise
But I got too close
Cuz when I tried to take the emotions further
I kept getting the cold shoulder
She told me one thing and did another
Then she went around and fucked with my brother
That was in high school, so I guess it wasn't serious
I still believed in love just in case you were curious
Moving on to my first real love, lyssa
Together for five years but all I did was kiss her
She kept me waiting for sex, which is not a big deal
It bothered me a little, but I loved how she made me feel
False validation she gave, she knew how to act

Found out she was fucking mad dudes behind my back
Once again I fell for the bullshit
If I was a psycho, she would've gotten the full clip
Finally after giving up I met an angel
She was sweet, cute, short and her hair was tangled
She told me she wanted me and couldn't wait
We intertwined our thighs after the 3rd date
Still sad to this day that I fucked that up
Made one mistake and she left
Didn't even want to tell me why she was upset
The next 2 girls after that just used me for head
It's weird that I never learned my lesson
Because every time I pushed the issue
I'm called "obsessive"
Tried to play nonchalant
Can't do that either
So, I've parked my heart alone, running up the meter
The next 3 girls in my life were exactly the same
I keep repeating the same shit, I guess I'm insane
So, forgive me for being overzealous
I'm just tired of feeling betrayed and jealous
Overthinking this caused me to start over drinking
Hearts floating on water with holes that stop slower sinking
Insecurities and doubts, I got 'em
As I watch my dignity float to this bottle's bottom
So, I hope you appreciate the story
It's no one's fault but my own, so no need to feel sorry.

YOU YOU YOU

When we met, you were so into me
You told me you loved me first
But lately it's gotten worse
Have to beg for a kiss
I'm not sure how to handle this
Sitting next to you, but you're far
The words I want to say bring blood to my jaw
Is there even any point anymore?
I've expressed it a few times, but you're clearly not happy
I wish I could make you happy
But I guess I can't, that's a fact. I'm sorry for this rant
I just have all these emotions boiling up
My heart and brain think she's toying with us
But maybe it's not me
Maybe it's just a result of my insecurity

SHOWER THOUGHTS

In the shower, tears on my face fresh
Reality's a mess, stressed
Funny how I can only write when I'm depressed
I tried writing when I'm happy but it's all blanks
Same with my shots, that's why I don't take them
Overthinking insecurities, I can't shake them
Took a break from love, now I'm confused
Forgot how to talk, forgot what to do
Making money now though, learned how to move
Self-love growing, not my time to lose
Relationships, I know, just got to show effort
Drunk, world spinning while I think of my record
The hearts I dismembered, the one I surrendered
That's all I remember

REALITY

Lately I've been scared to find out
If the facts match my doubts
Always running my mouth
But I have to express my feelings somehow
But I feel like you're real
Then again, this ain't a new feeling
Hooked on failure, disappointment I'm reeling
Using self-sabotage as bait, it's too late to wait
Self-fulfilling prophecy, an ideology I never left
Because if I expect it, it'll hurt less
I'm afraid of pain but I chase it
It's all I know, it's comforting to embrace it

DID I?

Did I finally meet you?
Or will it be the same pattern
Will you lift my heart out of space to Saturn?
Or will it be tossed aside like it doesn't matter
My insecurities showing, sitting on the train flowing
Heading straight into the dark tunnel without knowing
But something about you seems a little different
But maybe I want it so bad, that I'm tripping
I'm bitching, love, I'm missing, really wish I was sipping
Anything to get rid of this anxiety stalking
Because we'll end up texting for one day, then stop talking
Mr. Pain, I brought him along this path I'm walking
Maybe I'm being overly dramatic, my hopes feel like plastic
Get too close to the sun and it melts
The embers drip down on my sleeve and I yell
It's bloody cuz my heart's there, in case you couldn't tell

SUBWAY THOUGHTS

Got a girl's number, no doubt it's fake
I'll probably never meet the one, that shit I can't take
Try to forget about love, and focus on myself
At this point my heart's off my sleeve, it's sitting on a shelf
On my way from work, tryna gain money and lose weight
But it just transfers to my shoulders, all I can do is wait
Am I ever going to find her? I doubt it.
I shout it, if I know you, we probably talked about it
This dating scene is trash
About to go home wash away my tears in the bath
I'm mad,depressed and sad: How long will this last?
I can provide stability, loyalty, and effort
Then why am I in my pain, on the train coming from Bedford?
I spill my heart out into my poetry
Most people don't rhyme, I do, I call it flowetry
My ego's floating me, showing me that I ain't worth a thing
Constantly waiting for that phone to ring
Awkward as fuck, working on my confidence
Never know when to shut up, my tongue's a shedder
Honestly, I'm done with this night
I'm so lost, I don't even know how to end this right.

DEAR "DAD"

Dear dad, you finally called me today
It been a couple of months
I guess you remember that you actually have a son.
Always have excuses, always trying to front
Now I'm writing this poem, you have nowhere to run.
I just wish you would tell me why, just tell me all the feelings
that you have Inside.
I want to show you all the emotions that I hide
Thinking about it, joined by thoughts of suicide
But don't get me wrong I'm a lucky guy
I had a man take your place
The problem is we don't have the same face
I have a little sister that doesn't even know me anymore.
And it's really all your fault man
I have more things to tell you dad
So, let's take a walk, just listen, don't talk.
But of course us walking, is a figure of speech
You never have time, you never talk to me
You don't even care, I know you agree that I'm not your son,
I'm nothing more than a seed
But let me ask you a question

Why did you bother getting my mother pregnant?
When you never see your son, you never taught him a lesson.
Writing about you has become my obsession
I wish that my step-dad was my father, but that's not my
selection.
You're my first lesson of rejection, you weren't my protection
I have a whole family that don't know me
And it's all your fault
I can't say this to you since we never talk
So, I'm stuck dreaming about us at the park, writing this poem
while the blunt is sparked
From the start, I guess I just wanted to touch your heart.

THE VISIT

Walked in nervous as fuck
Got a wristband, but not going to a club
I was prepared for nothing except hurt
Took out my belongings, and gave them to the nice nurse
I was sweating like I ran a mile
But that all went away when I saw her smile
I sat down with a collared shirt, hands folded formal
She spoke to me, she seemed normal
She was okay and so was I
We played uno and talked as the time went by
I held her hand, something I had never really done before
I remember all the laughs we had since we were kids
The world changed, you're in pain and it's insane it led to this
You're going through shit but I'm here to help you with it
Times up, nurse called, now I have to leave
Hugged you hard, kissed your forehead, get better, please
Wiped my tears with my shirt, sorrow soaked up the heart on my
sleeve

NEVER GIVE UP

I like to think that I'm the perfect boyfriend
But I'm not
I'm a classic over thinker, I assume shit a lot
I feel a type of way about something, then I'm the one saying
sorry
See, I was hurt by an ex-girlfriend, it's the same old story.
I was with her for about 5 years
I told her everything, from my goals to my fears
Still, I wasn't the best communicator, so she cheated
Maybe I just wasn't something she needed
I know certain people will laugh, but we never had sex
She wanted me to wait, but she didn't wait with the next.
Till this day, I still blame myself
Tried to put those hurt feelings away on top of the shelf
But it just kept falling down
I felt like I lost my life, lost my world
After a year of isolation, I started dating another girl
Man was she great, had all the best traits.
She was more authentic than a fitted with the tag on
But I still ended up writing this sad song
See, after my last issue, I've started to over compensate
My emotions and feelings are all I would conversate
Overwhelming her with little shit
Took no time at all for her to dip
Once again, I blame myself
I think love is the hardest thing to do
Cuz you never know if that person really loves you

So, you trust blindly
Never knowing when your feelings are taken lightly
But I still believe in love
I see it all around me
Whether it be a parent and a child
Or even two friends who haven't seen each other in a while
So, shoutout to anyone who's ever been hurt
Maybe it happened because you trust too easily, or wear your
heart on your shirt
I want to say to you, I know how you feel
But before you cry and start fucking shit up
Just know that no matter what, you should never give up.

FINAL TOUGHTS

All my life I've been afraid of failure
So, my dream, I discard, it's just too hard
Fold my cards and blame my scars
I'm not good enough so why try
I'm okay with coasting by until the day I die
Telling lies, my grasp pointing away from the sky
It's rough to question everything, am I good enough?
Ran away from my problems, rather be safe
I'm the agency of complacency
If it's not broken, why fix it?
If I'm comfortable why change
I play what I was dealt, it's a fair exchange
NO!
I can't be this person anymore
My brain is sore, excuses I'll ignore
I can't be this person anymore
How can I expect to maintain love?
How can I expect to be successful?
How can I expect anyone to take me seriously?
I can't, not with that mindset
If you're reading this book, thank you
This process was scary, and I'll admit it
Even if it fails, I got up and did it